THE GEARHEAD'S GUIDE TO
QUAD BIKES

BY LISA J. AMSTUTZ

Raintree is an imprint of Capstone Global Library Limited, a company incorporated in England and Wales having its registered office at 264 Banbury Road, Oxford, OX2 7DY – Registered company number: 6695582

www.raintree.co.uk
myorders@raintree.co.uk

Hardback edition © Capstone Global Library Limited 2023
Paperback edition © Capstone Global Library Limited 2024
The moral rights of the proprietor have been asserted.

All rights reserved. No part of this publication may be reproduced in any form or by any means (including photocopying or storing it in any medium by electronic means and whether or not transiently or incidentally to some other use of this publication) without the written permission of the copyright owner, except in accordance with the provisions of the Copyright, Designs and Patents Act 1988 or under the terms of a licence issued by the Copyright Licensing Agency, 5th Floor, Shackleton House, 4 Battle Bridge Lane, London SE1 2HX (www.cla.co.uk). Applications for the copyright owner's written permission should be addressed to the publisher.

Edited by Erika L Shores
Designed by Heidi Thompson
Original illustrations © Capstone Global Library Limited 2023
Picture research by Jo Miller and Pam Mitsakos
Production by Tori Abraham
Originated by Capstone Global Library Ltd

978 1 3982 4841 0 (hardback)
978 1 3982 4842 7 (paperback)

British Library Cataloguing in Publication Data
A full catalogue record for this book is available from the British Library.

Acknowledgements
We would like to thank the following for permission to reproduce photographs:
Alamy: Amelia Martin, 8, Janet Griffin-Scott, 26; Getty Images: Jose Azel, 11; Science Source: Transtock, 29; Shutterstock: Aggie 11, throughout, design element, Artur Didyk, Cover, 13, Bilanol, 14, breakermaximus, 21, 24, diy13, 17, FabrikaSimf, 19, FOTOGRIN, 5, i3alda, Cover, luckyraccoon, 16, Maciej Kopaniecki, 6, 7, nikkytok, 15, Ruslan Malysh, 25, Sergei Domashenko, 9, 27, sirtravelalot, 23, 28, trek6500, 18, Vershinin89, 20

Every effort has been made to contact copyright holders of material reproduced in this book. Any omissions will be rectified in subsequent printings if notice is given to the publisher.

All the internet addresses (URLs) given in this book were valid at the time of going to press. However, due to the dynamic nature of the internet, some addresses may have changed, or sites may have changed or ceased to exist since publication. While the author and publisher regret any inconvenience this may cause readers, no responsibility for any such changes can be accepted by either the author or the publisher.

Printed and bound in India.

Contents

READY, SET, RIDE! 4

BUILT FOR SPEED 6

GET TOUGH 14

MAKE A SPLASH 20

    GLOSSARY 30

    FIND OUT MORE 31

    INDEX 32

    ABOUT THE AUTHOR 32

Words in **bold** are in the glossary.

Ready, set, ride!

Vroom! An engine **revs**. And it's off! A quad bike can handle almost any **terrain**. Its large tyres grip mud, snow and branches. Quad bikes are fun to ride.

Many people like to **modify** their quad bikes. They add **custom** parts. They use simple hacks to make their ride even better.

FACT
Quad bikes are also called ATVs. ATV stands for all-terrain vehicle.

Built for speed

Sport quad bikes are built for speed. They sit low to the ground. They are light and strong. The fastest ones reach 130 kilometres per hour! But you can make any quad bike faster with a few of these tricks.

An engine needs clean air to run at top speed. A clean filter lets more air reach and mix with **fuel**. This helps your engine run better. That means more speed.

High-octane fuel burns cleaner than other types. It helps your engine run better too.

FACT

Safety first! Always wear a helmet and goggles when riding a quad bike. It is best to wear long sleeves and trousers. Gloves and boots will protect your hands and feet.

Wheels also affect a quad bike's speed. **Stock** rims work well most of the time. But **aluminium** rims are lighter and faster.

You'll need to decide which type of tyre fits your needs. To increase top speed, choose larger tyres. On the other hand, smaller tyres can **accelerate** faster.

Rough trails are hard on hands and arms. A better set of grips can help. Choose grips with a waffle or **tread** pattern. They help to **absorb** bumps. They keep your hands and arms from tiring out.

Do your feet slip off the foot pegs in rain or mud? Try adding a pair of nerf bars. These webbed frames protect your feet.

Get tough

You're heading to rugged trails.

You want your quad bike to be in top form.

Try these tips.

14

disc brake

On steep slopes, you need braking power. Most new brakes work well. But if you have drum brakes, you may want to change them. Disc brakes are less likely to overheat.

Stock quad tyres have big grooves. Their rubber treads grip mud and gravel. But maybe you're headed to super tough terrain? Then you may want to upgrade. Off-road tyres have extra thick rubber. They have deep treads. They can handle almost anything.

If your ride is too rough, check your shocks. Maybe your quad bike has standard shocks. Then you may want to upgrade to fully adjustable ones. Tweak them to fit your size and weight. They will make your ride smoother. They will give you better control.

shock

FACT
The first quad bike was called a Jiger. It had six wheels and could drive on land or in water.

Make a splash

Want to really make a splash?

Give your quad bike some flashy add-ons.

Vinyl wraps can change the look of your quad. They cover the body like a skin. Wraps come in many colours. Some have camouflage patterns. Wraps look great. They help protect your paint job too.

You're out riding the trails. The only thing missing is some tunes. Problem solved! Just add a sound bar. It can stream music from your phone.

A whip light or flag adds style and safety. They stick up in the air. They help to make your quad easier to spot.

FACT

The Baja 1000 is a famous quad bike race. This relay race covers nearly 1,000 miles.

A light bar can add some flash. LED lights look cool. They make your quad bike safer too. Lights help you see better when it is dark or rainy. They also help other drivers to see you.

Tired of mud splatter? Add a windscreen to your quad bike. It will also keep bugs away.

You might even want to add custom seats or seat covers. They make your ride softer. They come in many colours and patterns.

You don't have to spend a lot of money to take your quad bike up a level. Buy or make some **decals**. Choose a design you like. Put these stickers on your quad or helmet.

Now you've got the coolest ride in town. Ready? Start your engines. And . . . go!

Glossary

absorb take in or soak up

accelerate speed up

aluminium lightweight metal

custom made to order

decal design printed on a sticker

fuel anything that is burned as a source of energy

modify change in some way

rev increase the speed of an engine

stock parts of a vehicle installed by the factory

terrain land or ground

tread pattern of raised lines on a tyre or other object

Find out more

Books

Cars, Trains, Ships and Planes: A Visual Encyclopedia to Every Vehicle, Clive Gifford (DK Children, 2015)

The Tech Behind Off-Road Vehicles (Tech on Wheels), Matt Chandler (Raintree, 2020)

Wheel Sports (Extreme Sport), Michael Hurley (Raintree, 2011)

Websites

www.bbc.co.uk/programmes/b0bpq7rd
Watch this episode of Catie's Amazing Machines about off-road machines.

www.dkfindout.com/uk/transport
Find out more about different types of transport.

Index

Baja 1000 23
brakes 15

decals 28

engines 4, 8, 29

fuel 8

grips 12

helmets 9, 28

Jiger 19

light bars 24

nerf bars 12

seats 27
shocks 18
sound bars 22
speed 6, 8, 10

tyres 4, 10, 16

whip lights 22
windscreens 26
wraps 21

About the author

Lisa J. Amstutz is the author of more than 150 books for children. She enjoys reading and writing about science and technology. Lisa lives on a small farm in Ohio, USA, with her family.